STEVE PIDD

RECEIVING TRUTH THAT WILL SET YOU FREE

Preparing the Pathway for ministry providing Healing and Freedom for; Spiritual, Mental, Emotional, Relational and Physical problems

ABOUT THE AUTHOR

Steve and his wife Em have spent the majority of their Christian life serving as Senior Pastors in a local Church environment. They have been involved internationally in training and ministering in the areas of healing and freedom for over 20 years. They have developed and conducted their 'School of Healing and Freedom' in various locations in Australia and across the World during that time. In more recent years their ministry abroad has mainly involved teaching and mentoring Pastors and leaders, as well as churches, to be equipped in the areas of healing and freedom ministries. Steve is the founder and International Director of Agape Orphanage Network Australia inc. For information on how to help children in need go to our website. www.aon.org.au

PREFACE

When Jesus walked the Earth, He noted that the people searched the Old Testament scriptures in the belief that if they learnt the right verses, that they would have a better future. However, without His work on the Cross that which they sought would remain out of reach.

John 5:39-40, "*39 You search the Scriptures because you think they give you eternal life. But the Scriptures point to me! 40 Yet you refuse to come to me to receive this life*". (NLT)

In much the same way, I have observed that modern believers search the New Testament in the hope of finding a verse that will set them free from their problems or bring healing. Yet these verses point to the work of the Holy Spirit. His ministry coming initially through Jesus, then the Apostles, and finally in our time through the gifts and ministries that He has placed in the Church.

INTRODUCTION

In 1998 we were ministering to a lady who was suffering with a fear. As usual we sought to find the source of her problem. God revolutionized how we saw ministry that day by setting her free from the belief that she held which produced the fear.

Since that time, we have seen multiple thousands and thousands of times that God has healed people of something that has troubled them in this way. This has happened consistently, week in week out over decades of ministry, with transformation, healing and freedom regularly being the outcome.

The types of problems that this ministry model effectively deals with includes; Spiritual freedom, emotional issues, relational disharmony, physical disorders, it helps with sexual adjustment, addictive bondages and many mental problems. It is 'a way' that God predictably sets people free through ministering 'truth.'

Copyright
Written and compiled by Steve Pidd
February 2020

All enquiries can be directed in writing to:
Steve Pidd
Email: contact@418centre.org

All rights reserved. This book is copyright. Apart from any fair dealing for the purposes of private study, research, criticism or review, as permitted under the Copyright Act, no part may be reproduced in any form (including electronically) without written permission.

THE HOLY BIBLE, NEW INTERNATIONAL VERSION®, NIV®
Copyright © 1973, 1978, 1984 by Biblica, Inc., ™
Used by permission. All rights reserved worldwide

THE NEW KING JAMES VERSION (NKJV)
Copyright © 1975, 1982 Thomas Nelson Publishers
Used by permission. All rights reserved

HOLY BIBLE, NEW LIVING TRANSLATION®, NLT®
Scripture quotations marked (NLT) are taken from the Holy Bible, New Living Translation, copyright ©1996, 2004, 2015 by Tyndale House Foundation. Used by permission of Tyndale House Publishers, Inc., Carol Stream, Illinois 60188. All rights reserved.

A more detailed study on 'Truth Encounters' can be found in the following books by the same author; YOU SHALL INDEED BE SET FREE is a study on the subject specifically. For further insights on 'Truth Encounters' along with teaching on the implications of deception in the Spiritual realm, as well as learning about the roots of common problems and how to work in ministry with the Holy Spirit, we recommend; HEALING AND FREEDOM THROUGH TRUTH ENCOUNTERS. All of these materials including additional units, which follow the School of Healing and Freedom format, can be found in the SOHAF COMPREHENSIVE TRAINING MANUAL.

CONTENTS

CHAPTER ONE — 9
What is the source of my problem?

CHAPTER TWO — 15
Romans 7 and the Apostle Pauls' Dilemma

CHAPTER THREE — 25
So how can I be set free?

CHAPTER FOUR — 39
What can I expect to happen in a ministry session?

APPENDIX ONE — 52
Sample Sessions

APPENDIX TWO — 59
Popular Redemption Scriptures qualifying us for healing and freedom

APPENDIX THREE — 62
Other Resources from 418Centre

FOREWORD

Having attended a great many conferences over the years, my observations are that the modern church is largely concerned with matters such as leadership, growing the numbers in congregations, or church planting. There is no doubt at all that these are wonderful and necessary topics to facilitate the building of the Kingdom of God.

There is, however, very little focus on healing ministries and as a consequence, doctors are the first port of call for physical problems. For many churches, even large city congregations, if there are mental or emotional issues, the people are sent to psychiatrists or Christian counsellors trained in secular techniques.

In contrast if we look at Jesus as the model, His focus was on healing the sick, freeing those with demonic bondages and healing the broken hearted. His disciples freely received this ministry from Christ themselves before they were commissioned to take the World.

*"Heal the sick, raise the dead, cleanse those who have leprosy, drive out demons. Freely **you have received**, freely give"* (NIV, Matthew 10:8, emphasis mine).

Perhaps we could look at it this way. Imagine if you were putting together a football team and selecting your players. "Alright, I choose that man over there with one leg, the blind guy, that deaf fellow, the man with one eye, those chaps with the back braces on, and those cripples." Then you launched them out onto the field, yelling with great enthusiasm and encouragement; "Go get them guys!"

It doesn't make much sense to me but many of us have been around churches where the focus is on trying to motivate broken people to live a victorious life of faith. We have all seen the fallout and problems from people with unresolved issues active in a church environment.

Remember the 'Vasa'

There is an old Swedish warship housed in a museum in Stockholm called by the name of 'Vasa.' She was commissioned to be built by the King of Sweden, Gustavus Adolphus, for use in the war with Poland-Lithuania. The boat was constructed between 1626-27. Upon completion she was considered to be one of the most powerful warships in the world at the time.

A tremendous amount of resources were put into her construction, and she presented with rich and ornate decorations. She was loaded with large and powerful guns. Unfortunately, all of the expense and efforts went into her appearance and equipment for war. Not enough time was spent on the design and what was done below the waterline out of sight. The result was that she appeared to be a splendid, dangerous and formidable enemy, when in fact she was unstable in her foundation and not well ballasted. The guns had just been fired as a grand salute to onlookers as the vessel left Stockholm. Sadly only 1400 meters into her maiden voyage she encountered a gust of wind which caused the ship to capsize and sink.

The lesson seems to be that if we spend all of our time on presentation, and how things look, and neglect dealing with the sub-surface problems of the church, we may not even get into battle. If we train people in leadership and develop or release gifts but don't deal with the unresolved issues in their lives, are we building on sand?

We have found that if we focus on people being set free, the gifts and leadership come with a motivation that God is pleased to bless. At times I have ministered to leadership teams of larger churches and have been amazed at what is going on in the background. I thoroughly believe that healing the broken-hearted and setting the captives free was the main ministry of Jesus for a very good reason. If we want to be the church that God is pleased to anoint, we may need to consider spending a little more time on working below the water line and sorting out the areas that are not always visible.

CHAPTER ONE
What is the source of my problem?

What are emotions?

What we know as Emotions or feelings are primarily a chemical and electrical elaboration of a thought or belief. It's how we feel our beliefs and consequent thoughts in our physical bodies.

This is mediated largely through our built-in electrical system or central nervous system. Working along with this we have the chemical release of hormones or neurotransmitters via our endocrine system, which allows you to know these emotions in your body. Emotions, feelings, even reactions and responses to a situation or stressor therefore are a reliable way to analyse what you believe or are thinking.

Therefore, what we would term negative emotions would include unwanted thoughts, responses, reactions and behaviour. They are predictable, and based on what you already think or believe. It's important to know that a feeling is rarely just a random emotion coming from nowhere, it is normally coming from something that you are thinking, often unconsciously, and this is the key to healing. So, we could say that feelings follow thoughts, and are the chemical/electrical response to these thoughts. For example, if you think about your favourite food your body will begin to release the hormones implicated in the digestive process. It won't be very long before your stomach is rumbling.

Emotionally we're the same. What we think or believe either consciously or unconsciously will precipitate the release of the corresponding hormones to make these thoughts a reality in our bodies.

Note: Because these feelings are produced by hormones, we acknowledge that at times there are other factors that can affect the balance of these chemicals, and consequently how you feel. For example, prescription medication, or to some extent tiredness or perhaps, for example a woman's menstrual cycle (usually these moments of weakness allow the inner beliefs that are present to come to the surface.) However, the vast majority of times emotions that are present will be belief driven.

Samples of negative thoughts and emotions usually stemming from inner beliefs would include issues such as; anxiety, fear, stress, resentment, anger, bitterness, guilt...self-rejection, fear of rejection, self-anger, low self-image, inferiority, worthlessness and so on.

These negative emotions do not match where we want to be, in terms of the Biblical ideals of positive beneficial feelings such as joy and peace. They are implicated in bad relationships, removing our sense of wellbeing, and finally even in destroying our health. As we have already pointed out the final activity of these thoughts and feelings is an effect on the body. This works in both directions. Positive conscious or inner thoughts and feelings have a beneficial effect on your health, and negative ones produce undesirable outcomes. A sample of this in scripture would be the following verse from the book of Proverbs;

Proverbs 17:22
A cheerful <u>heart</u> is good medicine, but a crushed spirit dries up the bones. NKJV (Emphasis mine)

The protective cells of your immune system are made in your bone marrow. So, if you have negative beliefs about yourself as a result of how you have been dealt with in life, it will affect your bodies defence system against physical maladies.

So, what is the heart? And where do these negative thoughts, beliefs, and emotions come from?

According to the very reputable Strong's concordance, we can see from the Old Testament word 'Leb' that 'heart' is translated from, literally means: 'an effect on your intellect proceeding from your centre, that produces feelings and has actions on your will and decisions;'

*3820. **Leb**, the heart; also used (fig.) very widely for the feelings, the will and even the intellect; likewise, for the centre of anything: Strong's Concordance*

Similarly, in the New Testament we see the 'heart' being translated from the Greek word, 'kardia,' as 'thoughts and feelings from your centre or middle.'

*2588. **kardia**, the heart, i.e. (fig.) the thoughts or feelings the middle:-(+ broken-) heart (-ed). Strong's Concordance*

Does it hold up in scripture that there is another place that holds thoughts and feelings, that is not your mind? It is clear in scripture that the mind is separate from the heart, and performs a different function. Your mind is your reasoner, your computer, it is like a screen where you view things to work them out. The mind holds information that we have voluntarily decided to try to retain such as scriptures or the ten times table.

Luke 10:27
He answered: "Love the Lord your God with all <u>your heart</u> and with all your soul and with all your strength and with all <u>your mind</u>" NIV (Emphasis mine)

Once we begin to understand and accept that our 'heart' is another place from where thoughts and feelings emanate, then we begin to realize that our problem may not be in the deliberate thinking that we do in our minds. Or for that matter what we know from voluntary learning in our minds. In fact, clearly many of our problems come from this other contrary set of beliefs, that are often in opposition to what we choose to know and believe.

The following passage confirms that the word of God exposes the not so obvious thoughts, and corresponding attitudes that proceed from our hearts and not our minds....and this is an area relating to the problems that we deal with which is largely untouched in the modern church. Consequently, many people retain their issues and unwanted behaviour, even though it is not in line with what they consciously think, know, or want to believe. It is against how they desire to feel, respond or act. We'll take up further explanation of this from Romans Chapter 7 in just a moment.

Hebrews 4:12
*For the word of God is living and active. Sharper than any double-edged sword, it penetrates even to dividing soul and spirit, joints and marrow; it judges the <u>thoughts and attitudes of</u> **the heart**. NIV (Emphasis mine)*

From a Biblical perspective these thoughts and feelings coming from our 'hearts' have implications regarding every area of life. Thoughts, feelings, decisions, motivations, relationships, health...absolutely everything. The Bible clearly states that above everything else what goes into and programs the 'heart' must be protected.

Proverbs 4:23
Above all else, guard your heart, for it affects everything you do. NLT (in part, guard the beliefs that you arrive at in your centre)

Possibly the biggest influencer, and most problematic area that needs to be dealt with when we are discussing 'heart beliefs' is those to do with our identity. What we think about ourselves, and how we think others see us, all affect our relationships with others, ourselves, and even God. These inner beliefs become the strongest predictor of behaviour and how we choose to live, act and react.

Proverbs 23:7
For as he thinks in his heart, so is he. NKJV

Once again in the preceding passage it is the thoughts of the 'heart' that depict the state of being of the man, and not necessarily his head knowledge. As you read your Bible you will begin to see that it indicates consistently that this is where many of our problems begin from. King David in Psalm 51 acknowledged that the reason for his wayward behaviour and sin was a lack of pure thoughts and feelings from his centre. And he requested that God show him what was there.

Psalm 51:10
Create in me a pure <u>heart</u>, O God, and renew a steadfast spirit within me. NKJV (Emphasis mine)

Psalm 139:23-24
[23] Search me, O God, and know my <u>heart</u>; test me and know my thoughts. [24] Point out anything in me that offends you, and lead

me along the path of everlasting life. NLT (Emphasis mine – 'heart' = thoughts and feelings from your inner parts)

Interestingly, and we will cover this in more detail in a moment, he stated that God wanted truth in the inner parts (Hebrew)....which in Greek is the soul. The soul is considered to be the mind, will, and emotions.

According to Hebrew scholars 'the inner parts' could also be translated, as the 'heart,' which I suggest to you is the centre or middle of your soul.

Psalm 51:6
Surely you desire truth in the inner parts. NKJV

Another example of the source of our problems being the 'thoughts and feelings from our centre, or heart' would be the all too common issue of depression. The scriptures lay blame at this inner place as being at the root of the problem. We have seen depression consistently healed as we accept that 'heart beliefs' are the source of the problem, and minister along those lines.

Proverbs 12:25
Anxiety in the heart of man causes depression. NKJV (by implication- anxiety from your inner central beliefs and feelings)

So, if we accept that the 'heart' is thoughts and feelings from our centre or middle, then what does a 'broken-heart' mean? We could perhaps best present it as thoughts and feelings that are broken or distorted. In other words, we have distorted beliefs, mainly about our identity, that are not in the order, or in the state of wholeness that God intended. Our identities are broken down and need to be restored, and this is the most common source of our problems. In the following passage we see that the Spirit of the LORD is on Jesus (and now the Church) to preach the good news...which is that you can be saved, but also you can have a better life now on Earth as well.

Jesus confirms this explaining that He is not just going to talk about Gods good news, but also demonstrate it. In order, the first thing that He is going to do is bring wholeness to the broken thoughts and feelings of the heart. The Greek word used here for heal is 'iaomai,' which means 'heal, make whole.' We have seen over many years that the result of this is the captives being set free, and spiritual oppression being broken.

Luke 4:18
The Spirit of the LORD is upon Me, Because He has anointed Me To preach the gospel to the poor; He has sent Me to heal the brokenhearted, To proclaim liberty to the captives And recovery of sight to the blind, To set at liberty those who are oppressed; NKJV (Emphasis mine)

CHAPTER TWO
Romans 7 and the Apostle Pauls' Dilemma

The Apostle Paul acknowledged that his unwanted behaviour, responses and reactions were coming from another law - (set of rules on how to live) - that he had arrived at, and now lived from, which were contrary to what he wanted to now do as a result of his spiritual rebirth.

Even though he was born again and he had a new spirit within producing new desires, he admitted that this previous programming was still active and 'living' within him, even though he did not want it. He came to the conclusion that this sin producing behaviour was something coming from an area of his life that he did not fully understand. This battle going on inside made him feel wretched.

In order to place what is happening with Paul in context, we need to realize that as a result of him being born again and experiencing regeneration of his human spirit, that this new connection with God produced conflict with the old ways. He evidently struggled with the previous programming of the inner thoughts and feelings from his 'heart.' He had received redemption, and consequently knew that he was now right with God, and was now aware of being in relationship with him. In Hebrews chapter 10 we see that as a direct result of redemption we have been made perfect (past tense) through Jesus' sacrifice on the cross.

Hebrews 10:14
For by one offering He has perfected forever those who are being sanctified. NKJV

Perhaps a good picture of this is the Old Testament story of Israel being brought out of Egypt. In delivering them from the control of their oppressors God did everything, and they did nothing. In the same way, in redemption, Jesus does everything and we do nothing. But then He led them to the promised land, which exposed in them the wrong believing about both God and themselves. Even though God had promised them victory, their wrong beliefs about Him did not allow them to trust Him and have faith. They also considered themselves as 'grasshoppers,' in other words, very small in their own eyes. This belief about themselves was formed through growing up as slaves, and as a result feeling inferior and inadequate.

So, we could summarize this as; Redemption = Jesus does everything in positionally setting you free and making you right with the Father.

Sanctification = the process of the Holy Spirit showing you what you believe in your 'heart' about yourself, about how others see you, and about how God regards you. We can, like the Israelites, identify these wrong beliefs from the negative thinking, feelings and decisions that our circumstances produce.

The process of cooperating with God in Sanctification

For modern believers, we note that we are in the process of sanctification as an ongoing ministry of the Spirit of Truth......who leads us into all truth. Jesus prayed to the Father that He would sanctify us through the Truth. An element of holiness then could be seen in the process of sanctification, and in being separated from thinking that is not of God, or not in line with Gods truth.

John 17:17
Sanctify them by Your truth. Your word is truth. NKJV

In this context, 'your word,' means something said by God. The medium through which He does this, is a communication from/by the Holy Spirit via some means, making what God says real to us. He will also often relay to us a sense of the future destiny and purpose that God has for us.

John 16:13
However, when He, the Spirit of truth, has come, He will guide you into all truth; for He will not speak on His own authority, but whatever He hears He will speak; and He will tell you things to come. NKJV

We can be sure that this truth that He brings to us, mind and heart, will set us free.

John 8:32
And you shall know the truth, and the truth shall make you free. NKJV

And so, we conclude that we are perfected and receive a new human spirit through Christs work, but that the new sanctified heart is a process, by the work of the Holy Spirit. God even promises that He will put His Holy Spirit in us, joined to our new human spirit. We understand this promise to be the baptism of the Holy Spirit.

Ezekiel 36:26-27
26 And I will give you a new heart with new and right desires, and I will put a new spirit in you. I will take out your stony heart of sin and give you a new, obedient heart. 27 And I will put my Spirit in you so you will obey my laws and do whatever I command. NLT

We can conclude that a 'new heart' means largely that we will have <u>new</u> beliefs, thoughts, emotions, feelings and motivations from our centre.

Returning to the Apostle Pauls dilemma in Romans 7, we can also see from the preceding passage that he now has a softened heart, with a new desire to be obedient. And God's Spirit within him is influencing him towards following His commands. It's noteworthy that Strong's concordance cites that an element of the Greek word 'Charis,' which is translated 'grace,' includes a 'divine influence on the heart.' So, Gods graciousness, along with covering our sins, includes putting in us a desire to cooperate with Him, and move towards establishing His ways and nature in our lives.

Prior to conversion there is nothing in opposition to our fallen self-centredness. We're in a sense our 'own gods,' only interested in doing our own will. Remember in the garden of Eden that a part of the temptation that Adam and Eve succumbed to was to be like God. This would mean that you rule over self and answer to nobody, because in your own thinking you are the central being. But after conversion we have this new God acknowledging nature in us. We still have to work with the Holy Spirit to deal with the old nature, or 'Sarx' as it is known in the Greek language. This process means dying to the old things that we lived for, primarily self-realization and self-pleasing.

Sometimes 'Sarx' is translated as the 'sinful nature' or the 'flesh.' I like to summarize it as 'the fallen self-life.' That is, the nature driven and empowered by programmed beliefs that are in line with fallen self-centred beliefs and perceptions. These are not in line with the truth of God and produce responses, feelings and actions that we may think will meet our needs, but are in fact sin. In Galatians chapter 5 and verses 19-21 we see the sorts of results or fruits of this inner thinking, and we note that all of the things listed are to do with self-gratification and getting for yourself what you think you need.

In other words, they are all about the 'fallen self,' how you can please your body or engender self-realization and self-promotion. In contrast, verses 22-23 speak of the fruit of laying down your will, and the fruit of the work of the Spirit of truth establishing His influence in us. As we examine this fruit, virtually all of these attributes are what you can give to others, and not what you can get for yourself.

Over the years we have seen as people allow the Holy Spirit to restore their identity by bringing truth to the inner parts, they become less and less concerned about their selves, and more and more wanting to serve others. This is I believe is a significant part of 'the being conformed to the likeness of Christ,' that we see in Romans chapter 8:29.

The example of these 2 natures working in the Apostle Paul

In order to be able to understand the passage in Romans chapter 7 we need to see that Paul has conflict within himself, as all Christians do. This problem is between the old programmed 'heart beliefs' powering the old nature, and the new 'mind-based beliefs' that are now learnt and desired through the influence of the new nature that God has created in us. As we examine the passage, when we're talking about the 'new nature' I will highlight it in bold. When we see that he is talking about his 'old fallen nature,' we'll underline it to make the distinction. Remember, he is one person, with 2 natures or sources of thinking influencing him. These are in opposition to each other. (Galatians 5:17)

Romans 7:14-16
*¹⁴ The law is good, then. The trouble is not with the law but with me, because I am sold into slavery, with sin as my master. ¹⁵ I don't understand myself at all, for I really want to do what is right, but I don't do it. Instead, I do the very thing I hate. ¹⁶ I know perfectly well that what I am doing is wrong, and **my** bad conscience shows that I agree that the law is good.*

As is the case with most of us who are now in relationship with God, the issue is not about whether or not we want to follow Gods ways, because His kindness has led us to repentance. (Repentance in Greek = a change of thinking, a reconsidering of our ways.)

Romans 7:17-19
¹⁷ But I can't help myself, because it is sin inside me that makes me do these evil things. ¹⁸ I know I am rotten through and through so far as my old sinful nature is concerned. No matter which way I turn, I can't make myself do right. I want to, but I can't. ¹⁹ When I want to do good, I don't. And when I try not to do wrong, I do it anyway.

I hope that the illustration is demonstrating his recognition of the 2 opposing influences within him, and the switch from one nature to the other. Much of his negative behaviour is coming from a pre-set 'default position.' This is stemming from previous conclusions and interpretations regarding his identity, and consequent perceived needs and desires to resolve these inner beliefs. Additionally, this would extend to how he regards what the world offers for self-pleasing the body as well. The 'old nature' is distorted by exposure to a fallen world, both soul and body, whereas the 'new nature' is influenced by a reborn spirit.

Romans 7:20
But if I am doing what I don't want to do, I am not really the one doing it; the sin within me is doing it.

If you are working in the garden and you get a prickle from a Cactus bush in your hand, you now have a prickle in you. Are you a prickle? No. You have been breached by something that you have been exposed to. For us, before being converted we were exposed to a fallen World with no defence against it.

As a result, some of the Satan manipulated world is in us. It is not us, even though we have been infected by it. Jesus said; "Father, forgive these people, because they don't know what they are doing." In other words, they are following what they have been exposed to, programmed by it, and do not know why they are doing what they are doing. Ungodly behaviour and sin because of the deception is the result.

Romans 7:21-25
[21] *It seems to be a fact of life that when I want to do what is right, I inevitably do what is wrong.* [22] *I love God's law with all **my** heart. (NKJV the Inward man)* [23] *But there is another law at work within me that is at war with **my** mind. This law wins the fight and makes me a slave to the sin that is still within me.* [24] *Oh, what a miserable person I am! Who will free me from this life that is dominated by sin?* [25] *Thank God! The answer is in Jesus Christ our Lord. So you see how it is: In **my** mind I really want to obey God's law, but because of my sinful nature I am a slave to sin.* NLT

And so it is with all of us. The true self inside of us, the reborn human spirit now influenced by the Holy Spirit wants to follow and obey Gods law. (Law = system of rules regulating actions, that indicate correct behaviour or procedures) But as with the Apostle Paul we have another law – system of rules governing how we act – proceeding from our prior programming and wrong beliefs. These have made us a slave to sin, which is ways of behaving or attitudes that are offensive to God. (Sin in the Hebrew and Greek languages means 'an offence.')

So, if the premise of our problem is wrong beliefs from deception in the old 'fallen self-nature,' then it is reasonably obvious that Gods truth leading to right believing in the 'heart,' is the answer to align us with a renewed mind. Paul agreed that some of his behaviour and the wretchedness that he consequently felt, was an area of his being that was not in order with Gods ways, in terms of how he should think, feel and act.

The 'heart' and the source of sin

Jesus clearly pointed to the 'heart' as being the source of unwanted, undesirable, and sinful behaviour. These are things that do not measure up to the word of God and the fruit of freedom by the work of the Holy Spirit. In other words, the choices, decisions and actions that are made to supposedly resolve, or be a solution to our negative beliefs and emotions, are influenced by the thoughts of our 'heart.'

Mathew 15:19
For from <u>the heart</u> come evil thoughts, murder, adultery, all other sexual immorality, theft, lying, and slander. NLT (Emphasis mine)

Remember that the 'heart' means the thoughts and feelings influencing your will from your centre or middle. We can be reasonably confident that a large part of this sin that was in Paul came from unresolved, wrong 'heart beliefs' that were in tension with the truth of God. The gospel of Mark adds some issues to the list. I am sure that many additional items could be catalogued. Indeed, we have personally witnessed that a great many sin issues proceed from the 'heart.'

Mark 7:20-23
[20] And then he added, "It is the <u>thought-life</u> that defiles you. (He is again indicating the thought life of the heart.) [21] For from <u>within</u>, out of a person's <u>heart</u>, come evil thoughts, sexual immorality, theft, murder, [22] adultery, greed, wickedness, deceit, eagerness for lustful pleasure, envy, slander, pride, and foolishness. [23] All these vile things come from <u>within</u>; they are what defile you and make you unacceptable to God." NLT (Emphasis mine)

Clearly through redemption we have now been made acceptable to God. But prior to this amazing gift our old thinking separated and put us against Him.

Colossians 1:21-22
[21] This includes you who <u>were once</u> so far away from God. You were <u>his enemies</u>, separated from him by your <u>evil thoughts and actions</u>, [22] yet now he has brought you back as his friends. He has done this through his death on the cross in his own human body. As a result, he has brought you into <u>the very presence of God</u>, and you are <u>holy and blameless</u> as you stand before him <u>without a single fault</u>. NLT (Emphasis mine)

*For further study there are other popular redemption scriptures listed in Appendix 2 at the end of this publication.

Ministry to the 'heart' and the church

Including ministry to the 'heart' is perhaps an emphasis that has been missing to some degree in the modern church, most probably through ignorance. If we don't know what to do, or know what we're meant to do, we tend to gravitate towards religion, which is what we know how to do and can control ourselves. The problem with this is that Gods people remain bound. In the following passage Jesus calls the Pharisees hypocrites (actors). They made a big show of the things that they did, but didn't have an emphasis on ministering to the people.

Today we often have entertaining church services, (which I enjoy!) but there is at time little emphasis on ministering to the issues within the people in their care. Jesus however indicated that we need to deal with what is happening on the inside as well, rather than only the appearances of the outside. In fact, at one time He directly stated that the Kingdom of God will be 'within you.' (Luke 17:21) At times He rebuked the Pharisees and the teachers of the law calling them 'white washed tombs.'

Mathew 23: 25-26
[25] *Woe to you, teachers of the law and Pharisees, you hypocrites! You clean the outside of the cup and dish, but inside they are full of greed and self-indulgence.* [26] *Blind Pharisee! First clean the inside of the cup and dish, and then the outside also will be clean.* NIV

At other times He took them to task for putting a heavy load on the people and telling them how they should live, but not lifting a finger to help them get free in order for them to be able to accomplish this.

Mathew 23:4-5
[4] *They crush you with impossible religious demands and never lift a finger to help ease the burden.* [5] *Everything they do is for show.* NLT

Some of our modern preaching is along these lines, telling people what they should do, but not setting them free so that they can achieve it. This is in contrast to Luke 4:18 where God promises to do the heavy lifting and heal the broken hearted and set the captives free. Believers need to know what to do to help people receive this ministry of the Holy Spirit. Sometimes this involves freely receiving ourselves first, so that we can freely give. For ministers, we need to realize that the people in our churches are not a part of our ministry, they are our ministry. We're responsible for helping them receive God's promises, whether we do it personally or bring in ministry gifts to facilitate the work.

CHAPTER THREE
So how can I be set free?

Where do 'heart beliefs' come from?

Involuntary or Experiential learning means in contrast to voluntary knowledge, things that you did not deliberately decide to believe or think of your own volition. I.E, It is conclusions not consciously made or reasoned, or necessarily computed in your mind and decided that you should deliberately remember. They have been interpreted from a significant event.... and generally, relate to your identity, (who you are) or a particular situation.

For example, if your father left home when you were a small child, then without wilfully trying to believe it, you unknowingly, and at times unconsciously through that experience come to the conclusion that you are 'not important.'

'Heart beliefs' and the importance of age

Proverbs chapter 22 and verse 6 instructs us that if we direct our children onto the right path that when they are older that they will not leave it. Biblically a child means someone who is pre-adolescent or under around 10 years old. The passage is instructing us that what is learnt at this critical age will decide our future direction and predict our behaviour.

Science bears this out, confirming that our brains are in a state of plasticity before 10 years of age. Coupled with this it is considered that this is the time where we are deciding who we are, how we are, how to respond to others, and subsequently how others perceive us.

Later as we go through life, we are interpreting new events through the lens of what we have already learnt and believe. It is therefore critical to realize that the source or root of virtually all of our identity-based heart beliefs will be found in memories interpreted at that time. At times it may very much seem as though that is not the case with strong feelings and beliefs emanating from later times.

For example, an event such as a marriage break up will be charged with emotion. It will appear as though all of those thoughts, feelings, and responses began in that situation. However, in reality the effect of the separation will most often reflect powerfully on your identity and bring up every negative thing that you have already believed about yourself, even though you may feel that the hurt it is coming from your partners behaviour.

The main Two kinds of beliefs that need to be dealt with

It is helpful to understanding the 2 main types of beliefs that affect us. These beliefs profoundly impact and predict our feelings, decisions, responses, motives and actions.

Identity beliefs - that is, beliefs about self

Identity beliefs relate to your perception of who you are and how you are. Rather than a lengthy discourse let me suggest some common beliefs reflecting how one's identity is seen. These inner unconscious thoughts have become lodged at the very centre of your being:

"I'm not loveable, I'm unacceptable, not enough, less than others, stupid, a nothing, dumb, ugly, a failure, a loser, useless, weak, I don't matter, am not important;" and so on. Notice that they are all beliefs relating to your identity, they are about your 'self.' You may or may not know them in words, rather experiencing them as a feeling or a reaction.

These types of *heart* beliefs are at the root of many anxieties. Unconsciously you are worried about people discovering your shortcomings or reinforcing them. If people treat you or regard you in a particular way, or you are exposed to certain circumstances, it may produce a predictable feeling or response that flags your belief. When I am preparing people for ministry, I often explain identity beliefs to people using a story which I have constructed, but is based on similar stories that I have heard over and over again.

Sample story

Imagine someone has come to you reporting how much anxiety they are going through. How I would deal with it may run something like this;

Fred: I have a terrible problem with anxiety.

Me: Can you give me an example of how it affects you?

Fred: I was at work the other day and heard the main door behind me open; I had an anxiety attack and reached for my pills.

Me: If you stop and think about the situation for a moment, what was it that you were worried about when you heard the door open?"

Fred: Thoughtful pause; Mmmmmm...I was nervous that it may have been the boss.

Me: And if it was, what are you worried about happening?

Fred: He may have come over and looked at my work!

Me: And if he did, what do you think could happen?

Fred: He might tell me that it was no good.

Me: I am sure that that is not a good feeling. I want you to close your eyes and feel what it is like for him to tell you that your work is not good enough, and let your mind connect you with other historical places where you have felt just like that.

Fred: *Pause;* I have just remembered that when I was in kindergarten, I was doing a painting with some other kids and the teacher was coming along looking at everyone's work. The first person was Mary and the teacher said that Mary's painting was so creative, and then Johnnie's was so neat and all in the lines. When she saw mine, she said, it was the biggest unrecognizable mess that she had ever seen in her life!

Me: As you look at that criticism and rejection, I want you to look for the conclusion and belief about yourself that you came to.

Fred: With some emotion; I'm useless, not as good as others.

Me: Let's ask the Lord what He considers to be true about you being useless and inferior. Just concentrate on those beliefs and feelings and listen.

Fred: *Pause;* He said, why would He have called and chosen me if I was useless. He said that all of His children are created equal, they have different gifts but none are better than another. I have just remembered that I was the best reader in the group!

Me: So how do you feel about people discovering that you are useless and not as good as them now?
Fred: Honestly, I feel that I am fine just as I am. And I am just the same as everyone else, the same only different, different in a good way, unique!

Identity beliefs also have a bearing on our relationships and how we respond, react to, and deal with others. They also reflect on how we relate to ourselves, and ultimately God. Truly, *as a man thinks in his heart, so is he*, in terms of how he reacts to others, and also how he sees himself.

Proverbs 23:7
For as he thinks in his heart, so is he. NKJV (Emphasis mine)

Situation beliefs

A 'situation belief' is a belief coming from a place such as a traumatic situation. It does not relate to your identity and 'who you are.' It is to do with 'how you are' in the event. Once having experienced it, it is now something that you are on guard against happening again. In a similar situation or circumstances, it now may produce unwanted stress, anxiety or even fear.

<u>Example Story: Two little boys</u>
In order to help people to understand situation beliefs I often use the following story when I am preparing them for ministry. There were two little 5-year-old boys walking down a street in their town. One of them noticed a motorbike across the road and went over to look at it. As the other boy continued down the road a dog came out of the gateway of a nearby house and bit him on the leg. In that moment of trauma, it was deeply encoded in him that dogs can hurt and frighten you. His mind has made a very good memory of the event, and he is now on guard against the possibility of it happening again. In order to counteract this ever-present fear, he reads numerous books about how dogs are man's best friend and that most of them will never hurt you. He is trying to counteract his involuntary heart belief with voluntary information from his mind.

This is often what we do in church and wonder why people never change or have limited growth. We give them lots of information to learn for their problems and tell them how they should think, perhaps sometimes not unlike the Pharisees. The Jesus model was to heal their broken hearts and set the captives free. I will explain what I mean by this statement a little further on, but back to our story for the moment.

As he grows up and becomes a teenager he is often invited to his friends' houses and really wants to go, but underneath there is a nagging hesitation and anxiety. He is not consciously thinking it but underneath the thought that there may be a dog at their house is producing the anxiety. So, his inner beliefs are beginning to affect his life choices.

Many years later the boys are again together walking and are now 40 years old. As they go along a small dog comes out of a laneway near them wagging his tail. The man who was bitten has an immediate physical fear response, even though with his mind he is trying frantically to apply the knowledge that he has about dogs and is telling himself how it looks so friendly. His *heart belief* that dogs sometimes bite you is greater than his *logical conscious knowledge* that the dog looks really friendly. The outworking is the release of fear hormones and a very uncomfortable feeling in his physical body.

His friend on the other hand has an entirely different response. He feels happy, warm and 'fuzzy.' What is the difference; it's the same dog? Growing up as a small boy, his family had a friendly dog that played with him, climbed all over him and licked his face. The emotions that he was feeling were coming from *different beliefs* about the same situation stored in his heart. So, the same situation was producing opposing responses based on what they already believed.

Traumas and Episodes

A real-life story to illustrate a 'situation belief' stemming from a trauma
A number of years ago we were conducting our healing school and a Chinese lady came into the session with her husband. All the way through the teaching she would cough every few seconds, not being deliberately disruptive, just unable to prevent it. The next day she made an appointment to be on the ministry list to receive some

help. As we interviewed her it came to light that she had been in an accident crushing her chest, and this was the beginning point for her coughing. She was a very brave lady and connected with the fear belief proceeding from the trauma, which was as I recall; *I am going to die.*

As she remembered the event and connected with *the belief and feeling,* we invited the Lord to bring His truth. In this instance, because she was connected with the event, a spirit of fear of death was exposed and manifested, and then came out. At the same time God communicated to her regarding *the trauma belief.* She was free and sat quietly throughout the day, finally testifying to her healing in the evening service. Also, she was healed and freed from some other problems, and as a result, was so pleased that she translated all of the considerable amount of school notes into Chinese for use in her own nation.

Physical healing as a result of resolving beliefs

As we have just described, many times the result of heart belief based emotional releases are changes in the chemistry of the physical body and subsequent healing. The body 'or outer man' is the end of the line in terms of your thought life. In fact, your disease or illness can often be a strong indicator of the particular negative emotion that you hold. For example, inner thoughts producing bitterness, resentment, anger or unforgiveness towards others or yourself will have outcomes that have been well catalogued.

The Bible doesn't clearly say how Jesus healed the broken hearted. At times it is described that many came to Him and were healed and delivered. There are different words translated as healed/healing in the New Testament. Two of the most common ones actually mean to be made whole. We could say then that people came for healing and freedom, and received what they came for by being made whole. This probably applies to dealing with the brokenness of the 'heart' more than any other area. Once the inner parts are in order, the outer parts reflect the same in health. Jesus most likely brought wholeness and then repaired the body simultaneously.

Example 1
Mathew 8:8
The centurion replied, "Lord, I do not deserve to have you come under my roof. But just say the word, and my servant will <u>be healed</u>." NIV (Emphasis mine)

The word for healed here is 'iaomai:'G2390 = heal, make <u>whole</u>. (Reference Strong's Concordance)

Example 2
Mathew 9:22
Jesus turned and saw her. "Take heart, daughter," he said, "your faith has <u>healed you</u>." And the woman was <u>healed</u> from that moment. NIV

The word in this instance translated as healed is 'sozo'= to save, deliver, heal or make <u>whole</u>.

Very often these passages include that people were healed, (which could mean being made whole) and also that demons left many. Without going into detail here, the ground that gives these evil spirits a place is often the areas of brokenness that people have as a result of what they believe in their hearts. In practice we have found that being set free from spirits is often the outcome of being made whole in regard to this faulty inner thinking. We can conclude then that this may well often be what is happening in these scriptures.

The example of a thyroid gland healed
A young lady in her mid 20s came for ministry with a presenting problem of her thyroid counts being, as she put it, *off the charts*. Her doctor was going to start her on hormone treatment immediately. I suggested that we work on the anxiety beliefs that she held that were producing the problem. We spent about an hour investigating and ministering to her anxieties. The next week she returned to her doctor reporting that she was well. His response to the blood test that followed was; *that can't be right, it is all in balance*. And so, he ordered another test which also proved to be perfect. An unexpected bonus from the ministry time was that she reported delightedly, that *the best part was that she didn't have a panic attack*, as she normally would when they did the blood test. Even her anxieties about the blood test were *belief* based.

A Broken Heart healed, leading to release from a physical malady
A number of years ago we were ministering in a large church in a rural city in Australia. A lady in her 50s was on the list to come for help and she was suffering from a variety of emotional problems. She was very eager to be set free and so her session went unusually quickly. Most of her problems were as a result of a considerable amount of sexual abuse in her early life. After around 45 minutes she reported that she was completely at peace and so we concluded our time together.

About 2 to 3 weeks later I received a message from her reporting all of the many benefits from the session. Unexpectedly she also reported that she no longer had to be hospitalized weekly for treatment to her liver and kidneys. I was not even aware that she had a problem as she had not mentioned it. Consequently, I had not prayed for her healing, it was simply a by-product of her broken heart being healed by the Spirit of Christ.

At times we deliberately target beliefs that produce disease, and other times it happens unbidden as a result of the healing and release from captive thoughts and feelings taking place. We have seen various problems, such as arthritis or asthma, being healed without direct prayer. Somewhere in the process of an emotional release, the body comes back into order and they simply disappear. That is certainly not to say that God does not heal the body in a number of other ways, it is a way that we see God healing the sick.

Accessing the Heart via the mind and emotions

How does it work? As we have already stated our sanctification is a process whereby we are separated from our areas of deception by the Holy Spirit bringing us Gods truth. The simplicity of the ministry is that as we become like little children and listen for the Spirit of truth to reframe our wrong believing, that we find that as one of His sheep we do indeed hear His voice. John 10:27

Because we have a society consumed with learning and knowledge, we often find a conflict between head knowledge and heart knowledge. People will ask us to tell them how to think, believing that they can fix the problem without God by using their own minds.

To date I have never seen anybody successfully do that, although many try for a time.

We access the heart beliefs by following emotion, or known self-beliefs back to the source in the heart.

Screens, icons, programs

For the sake of an illustration, let us imagine your conscious mind as a screen; perhaps as a television (TV) screen. In today's world there can often be up to 100 channels or more on our TV. On a normal TV set, you can only view one channel or program at a time. If I begin to talk about a hot dog or your favorite meal you may now have a picture on the screen of your mind. To access that picture of food you had to put whatever else you were thinking about to the side and change channels briefly. Your conscious mind is much like a computer in this respect, having been designed to be a sequential processor, or in other words to focus on one task at a time.

In a ministry session then, we are tuning into the fear, rejection or whatever other channel in order to view and connect with it. Thinking now of a hot dog, if we focus on it long enough, we will begin to have something happen in our stomachs as a reaction to the thought. In the same way as we begin to concentrate on, and embrace our fear or other issues, bringing them onto the screen of our conscious minds, we will have a chemical bodily response that we call emotion or feelings.

We can now begin to look for *the belief* and inner thoughts producing the emotion. Whether we present with a negative emotion and identify *the belief* producing it, or have a negative belief and let ourselves feel it, is immaterial. The important thing is that we connect them both on the conscious screen of our minds. Usually people will come presenting with negative emotions such as anxiety, fear, anger, rejection, bitterness and so on. Some people will look for help because of how they are reacting in relationships or to life.

As you listen to their story or problem you will most likely hear the beliefs behind the emotions come out in words. I usually have a piece of paper or a notebook with me, and record statements that

I believe may be connected to *beliefs*. Jesus said that we will hear the overflow of the *heart* from the mouth: Matthew 12:34b states,

*"... for out of the overflow of the **heart** the **mouth** speaks."* NIV, (emphasis mine)

For example, in the course of telling their story, somebody might say something such as; 'school was a difficult time for me, but that's not surprising, I can never keep up with the other kids!' When the time comes for ministry, we could say to them something along the lines of, 'I heard you say before that you can never keep up with the other kids; is that true?' Now, as they concentrate on that statement and connect with the feeling that goes with it, we can ask a further question to find out *the belief of the heart*. 'What does that make you, if you can't keep up with the other kids?' Their possible answer may be something such as; 'I must be dumb,' which is an identity, or if you prefer a self-belief.

The next thing that we want to do is find the place where they first learned this; the critical moment when they '*took it to heart.*' There is always a historically matching memory. They may report something along the lines of, 'when I was in grade 3, I could not do my times table and the teacher embarrassed me in front of the class.' So, I would probably say something along the lines of, 'so in that moment you believed that you are dumb because you could not do the times table?' Response 'Yes.'

Then I would say something such as, 'Lord, Fred believes that he is dumb and can't keep up with other people because he could not do his times table. His truth is that *he is dumb*; what is your truth for him?' As 'Fred' now has *the belief*, the matching negative feeling, and the historical event pulled up onto the screen of his mind it is time to ask God to reveal *His* truth to set him free. Whatever, God does in that moment will set 'Fred' free simply because He is God. The key for *us* in helping Fred is finding what is *believed in his heart*.

We tend to remember whatever is stored in the moment of emotional weakness and vulnerability. Surrounding details are not necessarily a part of interpreting the event so much as what is happening in the moment. God could remind him that he had been off sick and was not present when the instruction to learn those times tables was given.

Remember, this whole event including *beliefs* were beneath the surface in the heart all along. They needed to be deliberately accessed and brought into the conscious mind to be processed. It seems to be normally necessary to know what you believe before you can present it to the Lord to address it with His truth.

Dealing with multiple beliefs

Rounding out our illustration of a television screen, let us consider the multiple channels again. When we first began this ministry, people would come to us for help, and in a session, we might work through 2 or 3 *beliefs* and feelings that were a problem. They would usually report how free they felt, and we would be thinking that we had just worked with the Lord to fix up their whole lives! In some cases, people were happy with their new freedom, but many times we would be contacted with a report that they were struggling again. Upon investigation we would find out that everything resolved in the previous session was still settled, but there were other new issues. We have found this to be the case in ministering to others as well as receiving healing for ourselves. Most of us have a significant number of channels that need to be *reprogrammed*.

By way of example, someone may come presenting a problem of fear. They may have a fear of rejection, failure, flying, abandonment, or lack of protection or provision and so on. Each of these fears is *a different belief* and stem from various historical events. You can only have one of these *channels or programs* running in your conscious mind at a time. It is necessary to go through them one at a time and switch them off, individually, so to speak. You only need one fear program still running to feel, for example, anxiety. Typically, as you go through ministering to each belief the intensity becomes less and less until they are completely free.

That is not to suggest that every fear needs to be dealt with before your anxiety is completely gone. It is usually fear related to people that is ever present, such as fear of rejection. It is difficult to not deal with people as there are billions of them on the Earth. A fear of flying, for example, may produce no anxiety at all because you simply choose not to fly. However, if you have to fly for some reason, your *belief-based* anxiety will quickly be present and need to be resolved.

Computer screens

Most people today have seen a computer screen. We can use this as an analogy to further examine how our conscious mind operates. On most screens are little pictures called *icons* which have some kind of symbol depicting the program that they represent. The program is in the unit stored in a deeper place. On my computers you have to click a button twice with the pointer on the icon to open the program.

The point is that these icons connect you to programs that are there underneath whether you open them or not. In the case of operating the computer most of these are opened as a deliberate act. This can be the case with our minds. For example, we can purposefully open the time to cook the dinner program which holds all the information that we have stored and held as data about preparing food. It will come up onto our screen and we will access what we know to complete the task. In my case all there is when I open the *prepare dinner program* is, *'buy Pizza.'*

Critical events

The first time that we do anything is a significant moment in terms of encoding information about how we perceive that activity. Our early impressions of how we perform in areas such as the school environment for example, are a common place of memory where people arrive in a session. How our parents and teachers regarded and assessed our efforts will affect the way in which we view our person and ability to perform and meet requirements.

We could perhaps be compared to a sibling who is academically interested and gifted, and come away with some kind of inferiority belief or low self-image. Typically, these would be unconscious inner thoughts such as; *I am not as good as others. I'm dumb, a loser, useless, not like other people, a failure,* etc. etc.

This certainly has impact when we are deciding about our *identity* as a child, and while our brain is plastic and impressionable. Later in life we will use those beliefs to interpret other critical first-time events such as sexuality. Usually if the initial experience is not positive, they will see those activities through the filter of their existing *self-image beliefs*, having already learnt that they are *inferior or cannot perform as others can*. They will use these pre-existing beliefs to reach a conclusion about whether or not the activity is positive and reinforcing or yet another place for anxiety.

The Key

It is vital to understand and accept that many of the feelings and responses that you are experiencing are coming from inner thoughts that you are not necessarily consciously aware of.

We need to keep it simple, understanding that your role is connecting with your feelings and inner thoughts. Profoundly simple, but simply profound.

'The WHOLE ministry is pivotal on the principal that we are looking for, and trying to find, what you believe in your heart that you no longer necessarily remember in words.'

We could say that many of our feelings, reactions, and responses are automatized. By that I mean that they are not deliberate, but stem from conclusions and programming that has already happened. They are not a meditated and thought through response to the moment.

To explain this, if you can imagine that you have just alighted from your bath or shower and you begin to dry yourself with your towel. If in the course of the process you involve your conscious mind and think in your 'mind;' "do I dry this arm next, or this one?" You may now find yourself confused, and realize that you have interrupted an automatic preprogramed process.

In much the same way many of our feelings, behaviour and actions happen automatically without the deliberate process of thinking what our response should be. It is coming unbidden from prior programming, so that you don't know why you are doing what you are doing, or feeling what you are feeling.

Common beliefs, different personalities

After a period of time doing this ministry, you begin to find repetitively that there are some very common beliefs that you deal with over and over again. What does change is the differing personalities of the people that you are working with. Some people are very emotional while others have little emotion and are largely cognitive, mind-based people.

The key to the healing is identifying the belief, not the degree of the emotion. Someone who experiences feelings intensely may struggle with emotions daily. A more stoic person may simply get on with life but have issues, such as anxiety, or belief-based behaviour, such as the need to succeed, being regarded, or being right. The emotional person may have a dramatic time in the ministry session and express a great sense of relief and freedom.

The more cognitive person may only feel enough to identify and resolve the belief. They may not report much more than that the belief no longer feels true. Just because they lack the euphoria does not mean that they are not free. They are more likely to experience what has happened in terms of how they see life, their sense of peace and wellbeing, and notice that old responses and reactions have disappeared when certain stressors are present.

CHAPTER FOUR
What can I expect to happen in a ministry session?

Cactus bushes verses peeling an onion

Receiving ministry for our issues has sometimes been compared to peeling an onion. To me this suggests that you are dealing with multiple layers of the same thing. In reality I believe that it is more like pulling out the prickles on a Cactus bush. Each belief has its own individual root and source, although at times multiple beliefs may have been interpreted in one event. These are still individual in terms of how they may play out in life.

For example, you could have a number of anxiety, stress or fear beliefs that relate to different situations. Fear of failure, of death, of flying, of rejection and so on will each have a belief that produces the stress.

In much the same way you may have multiple inner identity conclusions that relate to inferiority, low self-image, self-worth, guilt, anger, fear of rejection, self-rejection, performance anxiety, depression and so on. Each has its own individual belief and source. These need to be ministered to one at a time as we bring them into our minds to process. We have found over the years that these are not endless, and as each one is ministered to you grow in faith, peace, health and freedom.

Most people have a number of critical beliefs that impact their peace, joy and wholeness. Some have had many damaging life experiences that have crushed and broken their identities and distorted their beliefs about themselves and life in general. Many of us need to steadily working on removing these 'prickles' to be completely free. Perhaps we have looked something like the diagram on the left at the top of page 40. Regardless of whether we have a few issues or many, God is committed to setting us free if we will set ourselves to present each belief to Him. In the end we look more like the picture at the top of page 40 on the right.

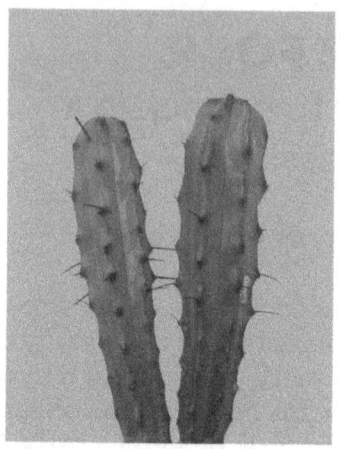 

It's worth noting that a major reason for Cacti having spines is to defend themselves from herbivores (an animal that feeds on plants). Once we have taken in a hurtful belief regarding our identity we often become, 'prickly' in terms of our perceived need to protect ourselves from further hurt. We endeavour to ward of those who could potentially touch or trigger sensitive identity beliefs about ourselves. We are on alert for those who may make us feel what we already believe about ourselves. Indeed, as a result of the rejection and low self-image that others carry, there will be those wanting to blow your candle out so that their own seems brighter. Others may want you to hurt because they hurt.

Some people process quickly, and others take a little time. What we have consistently observed, is that those who commit to the journey wanting everything dealt with, end up transformed by the ministry of the Holy Spirit.

Psalm 139:23-24
[23] Search me, O God, and know my heart; test me and know my anxious thoughts. [24] See if there is any offensive way in me, and lead me in the way everlasting. NIV

We have found over many years of ministry across the world that people may come from different cultures, have different personalities, but the beliefs that you find in hearts everywhere are 'common to man.'

What do I need to do to prepare for a ministry session?

Shopping lists
Note all Recent or current events, that are a 'stressor' or 'trigger' – or continuous negative feelings, beliefs, responses or behaviour – as the beginning point of a ministry session.

Also, once you are aware that your beliefs were first encoded in childhood, memories may begin to come to you. The fact that you remember them indicates that they were significant moments where you decided something and came to a conclusion. This interpreting of experiences is most often the source of a 'heart belief.'

From there we are wanting to concentrate on the feelings or thinking coming from beliefs in the 'heart' and identify the beginning place where the belief or conclusion was first interpreted.

As Jesus put it; 'Out of the overflow of the heart the mouth speaks'- the minister will be attentive to word 'cues' as they listen to your story or problem, as these indicate your inner beliefs.

By the time a person has read a book or listened to teaching on *heart beliefs* or has done a work up session, they should have a basic understanding of the ministry process. Many by now may have noteworthy memories coming to them. Anything that is a memory is significant or it would not be remembered to begin with. Few people can remember what they had for breakfast on a particular day 2 years ago; let alone many years ago because it really is not important.

We now ask the person to begin to put on their *shopping list* the areas that they may suffer with and are looking for freedom in. This can be known problems, such as never feeling that they are worth anything, or perhaps a fear of storms, or it can be a set of reactions that they have to specific situations.

A reaction example:
This may be something along the lines of; *I get very, very angry when my husband leaves his clothes on the floor.* This could come from some kind of belief such as, *nobody cares about me, and what I want.* A self-belief may be holding hurt behind that thinking, along

the lines of; *I'm a nothing, I just don't matter.* The *I'm a nothing* is going to be the identity belief that holds the emotional pain. The anger is not the problem but is a predictable response to being made to feel like this.

Their *shopping list* may contain a list of issues that they are aware of, and also a number of *trigger* circumstances. We encourage them to simply write down any situations that produce negative emotions. Anything that makes them feel angry, sad, fearful, indignant, rejected, inferior, unimportant and so on. A *shopping list* could look something like;

I just never feel worthy of being noticed. (Looking for historical match).

My husband always seems uninterested in what I want …..! etc. etc.

Some new ministers get nervous that they won't know what to do. As long as you remember that you are looking for *the beliefs that produce the feelings*, you are on the right track. We are not trying to give you methods, but rather principles. I am quite sure that my wife ministers very differently to me, but we are both looking for the same thing.

The people already have the problems so you don't have to find any. In addition, God has the answer for them already as well. Your job is only to help them find that which they *believe in their hearts*, then open it up to God to provide His truth. You can only minister to whatever they come in with to receive help for. You may discern other issues, but if they do not want assistance in those areas, then you acknowledge their choices.

The role of those ministering:
- To teach or instruct them in understanding the ministry.
- To help them identify and clarify the problem beliefs in their *hearts*.

If you are receiving ministry your part is:
- To be willing to seek out and note your issues.
- To be prepared to embrace, accept and allow yourself to connect with beliefs, emotions and memories.

The work of Holy Spirit:
- To guide and inspire the minister and person in the session.
- To reveal God's truth and bring freedom.

Note: At times people ask where this is in scripture, because they have not seen Jesus recorded as having ministered in this way. We have moved into the Holy Spirit dispensation, where Jesus prophesied that a work of the Holy Spirit was going to be to lead us into all truth. So, there is nothing unbiblical about this ministry. It is worth noting that other work of the Holy Spirit such as speaking in other tongues is not recorded until Jesus departed, and the Spirit of Christ began to work through believers.

The Goal

In John's gospel chapter 14 and verse 30 we see Jesus announcing that the ruler of this world was coming (AKA Satan). He was not troubled at his arrival stating that; "he has nothing IN me." Meaning that he had no sin that brought Him under the power of Satan through submission. And this I believe was because there were no wrong beliefs about His own identity, that is 'who He was.' He knew His mission and purpose in life, and about how the Father saw Him as a much-loved Son in whom He was well pleased.

Therefore, He was not vulnerable to any areas of deception that would cause Him to serve Satan as a result of His beliefs. He saw Satan perfectly for who he is, and what he was trying to achieve. This is where we are wanting to go in the process of sanctification, and receiving God's truth in the inner parts is our best defence.

Ways that God may communicate with people

An old saying says that *God talks how you listen*. He made your brain and soul exactly how He intended it to be. Some people think in words, others in pictures or impressions; let me offer some of the common ways that God might communicate truth to you. Remember the root issue here is that what we hold or perceive as truth is not a match with Gods truth, and so it is actually an area of deception.

1. In words:

I tend to think in words, so mostly when God uses my mind to communicate truth to me, it comes in words. Interestingly I have noticed that as I have become more and more free that I also receive pictures and impressions at times either for myself or others. Some people get stuck here because they are waiting for flashes of light and a booming voice, or an audible word from outside your body. I explain it this way. My computer is set up with the fonts, letter styles, writing size and so on that I like. If I were to give it to you and ask you to write me a note, when you returned it to me, I might exclaim; *that is just my writing!* That's true; but you just used my faculties or equipment to communicate your message to me.

In the ministry room, having identified the heart belief, I simply encourage people to let their minds go. When they hear something, occasionally people might explain that it just seemed like their own thoughts, but they heard this or that. We test and see whether or not it is God by looking at the old belief. Perhaps a person may have always thought that they were dumb. It felt true to them. Now they look for the belief and cannot find it, or it is no longer true; it has always been true to them, but it is gone.

2. Pictures or impressions:

Many people think in pictures. I remember a man who was suffering from a rejection belief of some kind. When this man spent time with his own children, he would put his face up against their face as a sign of love and affection, indicating acceptance and connection. The man was focusing on his belief and feeling that he was rejected, and God gave him a picture, an impression of the Heavenly Father putting His face against the mans. Needless to say, he was deeply touched and moved. In whatever way God chooses to communicate to us, it is in a sense like a *prophetic now word* from Him applied to our historical event.

In fact, I was ministering to a young man one day and as he embraced the *heart belief* that he held, the Holy Spirit took some words from a prophetic word that he had received a number of years earlier, and applied it to his belief, bringing healing to that area. Why did it not bring healing before? The young man did not know what he believed in his heart up until this time when we exposed it. Then the Holy Spirit applied the words to the belief.

3. Scriptures:

Very often the Holy Spirit will use a scripture that people know well in their minds and apply it to issues in their hearts. By way of example, I was ministering to a lady recently and she was in a memory where she was struggling to keep up with the other children in being able to do her school work. As a result, she had come to a conclusion and belief that she still suffered with daily along the lines of; *I am dumb because I cannot do the schoolwork like the other kids*. As she concentrated on the school memory and felt the belief, the Lord put into her mind the book of Ecclesiastes: *Everything is meaningless!*

For her, this meant that the activity that she was basing her identity on really did not matter. This brought her freedom. If the reference that she was measuring herself against was meaningless, then the conclusion that she arrived at had no basis and could not be true either. This was not a conscious act on her part to think differently, it was the result of the truth which the Holy Spirit communicated to her. Education is good, but it is a 'man' activity, and may not relate very much to what a person will be doing in life.

4. Realizations:

Several years ago, I ministered to a young man who came with the presenting problem of feeling as though he was responsible for everything that went wrong in his family life, his workplace, and even to some extent the world. As he connected with the feeling, we arrived at the place where he learnt a belief something like; *It's my fault if bad things happen*. As a small boy he was traveling in the back seat of the family car. They had an accident with another car as they entered an intersection. It was an emotionally traumatic event for the little boy. His father whipped around and said sharply, *have you got your seatbelt on?*

Now, it may seem ridiculous, but in that emotionally charged moment the boy thought; *This bad thing is my fault because I don't have my seat belt on!* These thoughts are burned deeply into our brains in moments of crisis through an electro-chemical process known as protein synthesis.

As we explored the memory, he discovered that afterward it turned out that he did in fact have his belt on. He now realized that the truth was that it was not his fault at all. He had believed that it was because, after the moment of shock, it was too late to reinterpret the belief that he had taken in when the emotional intensity subsided, because the belief was already in his heart. But now many years later the Holy Spirit reminded him of the complete picture and set him free.

Personally, I believe that one of the reasons that this ministry is so effective is that God dwells in eternity and not in time (Isaiah 57:15). He is everywhere all of the time. He is already there ten years from now, and He is there in your memory, whether you knew of Him or not as a child. So, we can identify the belief that you hold in this moment in time, and counsel you about it with minimal change. But when the Spirit of truth speaks into, and helps you reinterpret your event with His truth, He is actually there in your past!

Another example of a realization could be a child coming into a room where mother and father are having a heated argument. In that moment the child believes that it is somehow their fault. Looking back and exploring the memory through the eyes of God they now realize, as they see more of the picture that was not as emotionally intense, that the parents were already fighting before they entered the room. So, how could it be their fault? God will at times bring freedom through realization. I have also seen in other instances people being set free at the moment where they realize why they believe what they believe, and where it came from, and for them that is the healing.

5. Sensations, feelings, knowing:
God is indeed very creative in how He communicates with us. Normally we do not know what He is going to do, or how He will do it. Sometimes He will give us insight into what He is about to say or do. I think in part this is on the job training for words of knowledge and learning to hear his voice for ourselves.

I recall one lady who had suffered severe physical abuse, and as she was accessing memories and beliefs, there was a light coming into the picture. When the light came in, she felt peaceful, calm, and safe. I was frantically going through my theology to make sure that this was something Biblical. Remembering, Jesus, light of the world reassured me that this was something that God might do. The bottom line was that her fears were resolved.

Other people report simply feeling love. Still more report that they just know that the beliefs they held are not true. I remember asking one lady after a session what she now thought of God. She thought about it for a moment, and then replied; *He's clever, He's very clever!* Amen. Our God is indeed very clever.

6. Through our senses

One lady that we ministered to had come with the presenting problem of struggling to believe God for provision. She was actually a woman of great faith in most areas of her life. However, as a child she was never sure that they were going to have food to eat. The belief that she took to heart as a result of that anxiety was at the root of the problem. Immediately after we asked God to communicate His truth to her, she asked a question; *who has got the bread? I can smell bread!* After assuring her that no one had bread I asked her what the smell of bread meant to her. She reported that it meant that; *there will always be enough.* For her this resolved the issue, and as a result of her new expectations of God providing, over the next few months her family situation changed dramatically.

Through our senses seems to be a much less common way that God uses, but it happens from time to time.

By whatever means He frees us we can be sure that God is always about helping people. Whether we are receiving or ministering, He uses our time doing so to learn about Him, about His goodness, and this occurs as we see His love, grace and ability to help His children.

Warning

Many ministries have gone off the rails and brought this ministry into disrepute by suggesting how God should communicate with the people receiving ministry. Having identified and connected with the belief and feelings we have found that God is more than able to consistently do His part without our help.

Sample questions that can be used to help identify beliefs

As you begin to work in this ministry, or even examine your own thoughts, you will find that there are only a certain number of questions available to use, and I suggest some here. You can of course be creative and come up with your own.

"What will happen if ... ?" (e.g. ...'you have to fly overseas').

Note: We call fear the **'what if spirit!'** so **'what will happen if?'** is a good basic question for fear, anxiety, stress or insecurity.

"How does it feel to think that...?" (e.g. ...'there is nobody to protect you').
"How does this make you feel ... ?" (e.g. ...'to think that you don't matter').
"Why do you think ... ?" (e.g. ...'no one cares about you').
"What does this mean about you" (e.g. ...'that everyone else is able to succeed').
"What does it make you ... ?" (e.g. ...'if you are the person who is ignored').
"What do you believe is true about you ... ? (e.g. ... if someone has perhaps, learnt that they are stupid in an event).

Typical emotion/reaction producing conscious or unconscious thoughts

Fear/Anxiety: "This or that could happen!"
Anger: "They don't care about me!" "This is not how things should be!"
Rejection: "Nobody wants me, I don't belong, I am not a part of this."
Stress: "I can't cope!" "It's hopeless." (Depression)
Sadness: "I am not loved, I have missed out on or lost something I need"
Rebellion: "It's not fair!"

Performance anxiety
/ inferiority: "I cannot be enough, am not good enough, and can't do what others can do, or what is expected or required of me to qualify for acceptance."

Insecurity: "People aren't doing what they should be doing."

Bitterness / resentment: "I will not forgive them for what they have done" or at times, "what they have not done that they should have!"

All of these kinds of perceived beliefs affect relationships and often produce sin responses and reactions. For example; unforgivness, bitterness or resentment.

Common reasons why people may not come for ministry

1. Ignorance. They simply do not know about this opportunity for freedom, or they have received a distorted picture of it from some source.

2. Fit. It does not fit into their theological or ministry method framework.

3. Pride. Pride is the most common reason. Many people are full of their own opinions and views. Having some knowledge, they become *puffed up*. They want to fix the problem themselves without help from others, working it out in their own minds. Remember the Pharisees who considered themselves above the common sinners. Jesus at one time rebuked them for searching the scriptures because they thought that the written word alone would provide eternal life.

Pride says, *I will fix me!* in a sense, following on from the temptation in the garden to be *as or like God!* Pride wants to set up a monument to self to bow down to and be, in a way, your own god. Jesus pointed out that the scriptures actually do not fix you without Him, the word made flesh. He is the person whom the Holy Spirit can work through and meet your needs. The principle is the same for receiving the promise of eternal life, and also receiving other provisions that come through Jesus.

John 5:39-40
"³⁹ You diligently study the Scriptures because you think that by them you possess eternal life. These are the Scriptures that testify about me, ⁴⁰ yet you refuse to come to me to have life." NIV

The beginnings or ground that gives place to pride is found in inferiority and low self-image. Pride, or making yourself above others in your own thinking is the devil's solution for the perceived weakness that you hold about yourself at heart level.

Proud people are probably the ones who stay away from receiving help more than any others. Their behaviour, or how they appear, is often the exact opposite of a person's inner belief. For example, a person who walks around appearing self-important and superior almost certainly believes in their hearts that they are not important and are inferior. Now, the only viewpoint that holds any importance for them is their own. They will have the attitude that you better listen to them, and they often hold the floor in conversations. King Solomon was not kind in his appraisal of these hurting people in many of his writings.

Proverbs 26:12
"Do you see a man wise in his own eyes? There is more hope for a fool than for him." NIV

For a proud person to admit to any kind of weakness or imperfection strikes at the core of their sense of inferiority. And after all, what could anybody possibly know that they do not! The result is that many with pride issues avoid ministry. There can at times be an evil spirit involved in the resistance to help. Even if there is not a demon on the inside, pride certainly proceeds from spiritual influences even from the outside.

A while ago we had a new lady coming to our church who asked me if she could come for some help with her problems. She asked me if I could make sure that I don't tell the other leaders that she was coming. I replied with something like, *Sure, no problem. But I don't think that they would pay much attention, as many of the congregation comes for sessions and most of the leaders receive ministry themselves!* This seemed to put her at ease. The point is, isn't this what normal church life should look like anyway?

4. Control. We have already discussed that many people want to be in absolute control of their lives. For some of these persons, to be able to trust another with the deep things of their lives is very difficult.

5. Fear. There are those who are simply too afraid of what might happen, what you might think about them, or what they may have to face to consider opening up for help.

6. Denial. Some people simply will not accept they have problems, or that they may have a part in faulty relationships. These people expect that their own emotional well-being would be fine if everyone around them did what they think they should be doing. This is called *projection*, where you deny your issues and blame shift your situation, feelings and responses onto everyone else. It is not surprising that we see the first instance of not taking responsibility for our own behaviour right back at mankind's beginnings in Genesis.

Genesis 3:11-12
[11] And he said, "Who told you that you were naked? Have you eaten from the tree that I commanded you not to eat from?" [12] The man said, "The woman you put here with me--she gave me some fruit from the tree, and I ate it." NIV

APPENDIX ONE
Sample Sessions

Sample ministry to rejection beliefs scenario

A person approaches you for help.

Step 1: Explain the process to the person, and what you are looking for, namely *heart beliefs*. This process could include having them read, view or listen to material such as this explaining the ministry.

Step 2: The person comes for the actual ministry session.

Note: They already have the problem that they are struggling with so you don't need to come up with anything. It is not your job to fix their whole life, just try to help them with whatever is presenting at the time.

Listen to their story and the issue that they are bringing to you. Make notes of the things that they *say* that may be clues to what they *believe*. Writing things down is good as it means that you don't miss things that may need to later be visited, and you don't need to interrupt their story.

Step 3: Ministry Example

Fred: I felt very uneasy when I went to try out for the church choir!
Me: Why do you think that you were uncomfortable in that setting?
Fred: I think that I felt that I did not belong there, I was not a part of it.

This could indicate a possible belief such as; *I am not wanted*, or *I am not accepted*.

Step 4: We have them concentrate on the feeling produced by the thought that they do not belong, and are not a part of it; rejected by the group. We are looking for the earliest possibly historical place where they learnt beliefs that caused them to feel this way.

Fred: I have just remembered my first day of school. There was a group of kids playing and talking together and they ignored me!

Me: As you concentrate on the memory and feel that rejected feeling, why do you think that they ignored you?

Fred: *Pauses and explores the memory.* I think it is because I am not like them, I am new and so they don't want me. This must be true because they are all accepting each other, but I am on the outside!

Me: Let's ask the Lord what His truth, the real truth is. Lord what do you want Fred to understand about that time where he felt that he was not wanted because he is not like them, because he is new?

Fred: The Lord is reminding me, that these kids went to Kindergarten together and already knew each other. I couldn't get in to Kinder because they were full up.

Me: So, are you not wanted because you are different?

Fred: No, I am the same; I have just not built relationships yet. Later I did make some good friends there.

Me: How do you feel about the church choir now?

Fred: I feel excited about it now; I will be making some new friends it will just take a little time.

Me: Perhaps close in prayer thanking the Lord for His healing, or I may enquire as to whether or not there are other things which require ministry.

Clearly this example is not going to be as deeply painful as rejection often is. Some people may have very painful traumatic rejection situations from some kind of abuse or absence of love in the home. Other people may have a *profile of rejection* composed of multiple less painful beliefs.

Sample ministry: Situational or phobic fear

Me: "What can we help you with today?"
Fred: "Well I have a fear of flying."
Me: "So what are you afraid might happen when you get on an aircraft?"
Fred: Ponders "I feel as though I will be out of control"
Me: "I want you to focus on that thought and the feeling that goes with it and see if you remember a time in your life where you felt just like that."
Fred: "I remember being pushed down a steep hill in a little cart we had made. The big kids put me in and sent the cart racing down the hill towards the trees."
Me: "What did you believe might happen while you were afraid?"
Fred: "I guess I felt that I was going to get hurt and nobody could stop it happening. I was terrified!"
Me: "Let's hold that belief up to the Lord that 'nobody can stop what's going to happen, and I will get hurt.'" (Prayer asking the Lord to bring His truth)
Fred: "I just remembered that actually one of the big kids ran after me and eventually did stop the cart before it hit the trees."
Me: "So what does that mean to you?"
Fred: "Well it means that God will always find a way to protect me. He is always in control."
Me: "So think about flying now, are you still afraid of being out of control?"
Fred: Pauses "No. I am still a bit fearful though it is nowhere near as much!"
Me: "Alright focus on the residual fear and see if you can work out what you are afraid of."
Fred: "I have been on a plane before and it felt like there was nothing solid underneath me....it was a scary feeling."

Me:	"Okay, I want you to concentrate on the anxious belief that there is nothing solid underneath you." "Lord, would you help Fred to connect with a place where he felt just like that before?"
Fred:	"As soon as you said that I remembered being on a cliff edge when we were kids and it caved in underneath me. I slid down the face of it and into the river."
Me:	"So you felt as if there was nothing solid under you? And what was the consequence or fear expectation about that situation?"
Fred:	"I thought that I was going to die!"
Me:	"Alright, I just want for you to embrace that anxiety and belief in that memory that because there is nothing solid under you, you will die."
Fred:	Pauses "Do you know, that is just not true. What came to mind was the scripture that talks about the circle of the Earth. It's just hung out there in space with nothing under it just because God put it there and supports it, nothing under it, but still suspended."
Me:	"So if you think about there being nothing solid under you on a plane how do you feel about it now?"
Fred:	"You know it's really okay....!"
Me:	"How do you feel about flying now Fred?"
Fred:	"Do you know, it's weird but I think that I am a bit excited!"

Perhaps we might say a prayer thanking the Lord, or certainly make a comment about how amazing our God is in setting us free, and acknowledging Him as being the one who has done the freeing. Either way, God is glorified as He fulfills His promise and the session closes.

Sample ministry: Identity belief-based fear

Me:	"What seems to be the problem?"
Fred:	"I have been asked to do communion in church next Sunday, but I am petrified and haven't been able to sleep!"
Me:	"I want you to imagine yourself up there in front of all those people. As you feel that anxiety, I would like you to examine it and try to work out exactly what it is that you are afraid might happen."

Fred:	Pause "I am afraid that I might not be able to do it properly."
Me:	"I would like you to feel that anxiety about not doing it properly, and as you do let your mind connect you with a place that held those same feelings. It will be somewhere where you actually couldn't do what was expected."
Fred:	Ponders "I remember in school when I was about 7 years old. The teacher wanted me to write some cursive text on the blackboard, and I wrote it back the front. The teacher made a big fuss over it making fun of me in front of the whole class, and I recall being incredibly embarrassed."
Me:	"As a result of not being able to do it, and the intense embarrassing moment in front of the class, what conclusion about yourself did you come to?"
Fred:	Pause, thoughtful "I'm dumb. I must be dumb because I could not do it right."
Me:	"As you feel that embarrassment and the belief that you are 'dumb' because you could not do it, let us ask the Lord what the real truth is."
Prayer:	"Lord Fred thinks that he is dumb because he could not do the cursive writing on the board. What do you want him to know about that situation?"
Fred:	"Well, I didn't hear any thoughts. But I just sort of understood that none of us had actually been taught cursive yet. And the teacher liked to mock us and make fun of us. She sort of deliberately put me in that position to make sport of me."
Me:	"So are you dumb because you could not do it?"
Fred:	"No, the truth is that none of us could yet. I am feeling that I was alright, there is nothing wrong with me, but I think that the teacher had some issues. I forgive her."
Me:	"Picture yourself doing communion on Sunday, how do you feel about messing it up now?"
Fred:	"I actually feel fine about it; I will work out how to do it as best I can and really everything doesn't have to be perfect. After all, we are all family."

Note: A situation such as public speaking typically may evoke a response from more than one historically learnt fear producing belief. As each one is ministered to the intensity of the anxiety normally goes down. If you just process the beliefs one by one eventually you will achieve peace. It is of course normal to be a little nervous if it is a new situation.

- Appendix One -

Flow chart

The ministry process:
A person comes to you with a problem. This could be a mental, emotional, relational, addictive, spiritual, sexual or physical issue.
↓
They may have been *set off* or *triggered* by a life situation producing for example: anxiety, anger, sadness, bitterness, resentment, guilt, inferiority, rejection and so on.
↓
Your role is to help them focus on these feelings and reactions and to identify the beliefs which they believe at *heart* level, and which they may no longer immediately consciously access.
↓
The key components that you are trying to connect here are: The emotions, the beliefs producing the emotions, and the matching memory pictures. (No pictures could mean it's imbibed prenatal, perhaps connect with a feeling or a sense of something)
↓
You have them focus on the presenting feelings and using questions help them to discover the beliefs producing the emotion, OR
↓
If they have a belief, such as, *I just never think that I am good enough*, have them connect with the feeling that should be associated with such a thought. (The emotion often comes up as the story is related or the memory is accessed and described.)

In the instance of such beliefs as; "I am not good enough, not loveable, not important..." and so on a qualifying phrase can be helpful. For example, ask the question; "why are you not good enough?" You can then offer the belief with the qualifying phrase, such as: "Lord Fred believes that he is not good enough and <u>is dumb</u> **because** he cannot do what others can do."

The conclusion is that he is 'dumb,' but there can be many reasons why he may believe this. So when we offer it to the Lord for truth we make it specific by adding in the phrase that 'he believes that he <u>is dumb</u>, **because** he cannot do what others can do.'
↓
Request that they let memories come to them or wilfully look for the memory picture, if they don't already have it, which contains

-57-

the beginnings or original source of the thoughts and feelings. (With some pictures that are remembered, it is not always immediately obvious as to why the beliefs have been interpreted here.)

↓

Having refined and identified the belief that was learnt, invite God to bring Truth. (You can be creative in how you request this to avoid being repetitive, but using phrases such as, *Lord, would you like to show Fred how you see this situation? Lord, would you touch Fred by revealing your Truth to replace what he perceives as the truth here? Lord, what would you like Fred to know about the belief that he holds?* and so on.)

APPENDIX TWO
Popular Redemption Scriptures qualifying us for healing and freedom

All of the following passages are taken from the New Living Translation of the Bible and the emphasis is mine.

PSALM 103:2-4, 10-12
² Praise the LORD, I tell myself, and never forget the good things he does for me. ³ He forgives **all** my sins and heals **all** my diseases. ⁴ He ransoms me from death and surrounds me with love and tender mercies.

…….And………

¹⁰ **He has not punished us for all our sins**, nor does he deal with us as we deserve. ¹¹ For his unfailing love toward those who fear him is as great as the height of the heavens above the earth. ¹² **He has removed our rebellious acts as far away from us as the east is from the west**.

ISAIAH 44:22
"I have swept away your sins like the morning mists. I have scattered your offenses like the clouds. Oh, return to me, for I have paid the price to set you free."

ISAIAH 53:5-6, 11
⁵ But he was wounded and crushed for our sins. He was beaten that we might have peace. He was whipped, and we were healed! ⁶ **All of us** have strayed away like sheep. We have left God's paths to follow our own. Yet the LORD laid on him the guilt and sins **of us all**.

…….And………

¹¹ When he sees all that is accomplished by his anguish, he will be satisfied. And because of what he has experienced, my righteous servant will make it possible for many to be counted righteous, for he will bear all their sins.

ROMANS 3:22-25

²² We are made right in God's sight when we trust in Jesus Christ to take away our sins. And we all can be saved in this same way, no matter who we are or what we have done. ²³ For all have sinned; all fall short of God's glorious standard. ²⁴ Yet now God in his gracious kindness declares us not guilty. **He has done this through Christ Jesus, who has freed us by taking away our sins.** ²⁵ For God sent Jesus to take the punishment for our sins and to satisfy God's anger against us. **We are made right with God when we believe that Jesus shed his blood, sacrificing his life for us.**

1 CORINTHIANS 1:30-31

³⁰ God alone made it possible for you to be in Christ Jesus. For our benefit God made Christ to be wisdom itself. **He is the one who made us acceptable to God. He made us pure and holy, and he gave himself to purchase our freedom.** ³¹ As the Scriptures say, **"The person who wishes to boast should boast only of what the Lord has done."**

2 CORINTHIANS 5:21

For God made Christ, who never sinned, to be the offering for our sin, **so that we could be made right with God through Christ.**

EPHESIANS 1:4-7

⁴ Long ago, even before he made the world, **God loved us and chose us in Christ to be holy and without fault in his eyes.** ⁵ His unchanging plan has always been to adopt us into his own family by bringing us to himself through Jesus Christ. **And this gave him great pleasure.** ⁶ So we praise God for the wonderful kindness he has poured out on us because we belong to his dearly loved Son. ⁷ He is so rich in kindness that he purchased our freedom through the blood of his Son, **and our sins are forgiven.**

EPHESIANS 2:7

⁷ And so God can always point to us as examples of the incredible wealth of his favor and kindness toward us, as shown in all he has done for us through Christ Jesus. ⁸ God saved you by his special favor when you believed. And **you can't take credit for this; it is a gift from God.** ⁹ **Salvation is not a reward for the good things we have done,** so none of us can boast about it.

COLOSSIANS 1:22
"yet now he has brought you back as his friends. He has done this through his death on the cross in his own human body. **As a result**, he has brought you into the very presence of God, and **you are holy and blameless as you stand before him without a single fault.**"

HEBREWS 10:14, 17-18
[14] For by that one offering **he perfected forever** all those whom he is making holy

......and....

[17] Then he adds, "**I will never again remember their sins and lawless deeds.**" [18] Now when sins have been forgiven, there is no need to offer any more sacrifices.

APPENDIX THREE
Other Resources from 418Centre by Steve Pidd

SOHAF (SCHOOL OF HEALING AND FREEDOM) COMPREHENSIVE TRAINING MANUAL
This manual follows the SOHAF format and includes detailed studies of the School Units to help equip and instruct a disciple of healing ministries.

SOHAF (SCHOOL OF HEALING AND FREEDOM) BASIC SEMINAR MANUAL
This is the simplified study guide version of the manual. It is provided as a companion to notes for those attending SOHAF Schools or Seminars.

HEALING AND FREEDOM THROUGH TRUTH ENCOUNTERS
This popular book is a complete resource in itself. It contains much of the material found in the SOHAF Comprehensive manual. It is presented in a different order with the focus on explaining the 'Truth Encounters' ministry. It includes explanations on the demonic realm, roots of common issues, and how to work with the Holy Spirit in ministry.

YOU SHALL INDEED BE SET FREE
This publication is an excerpt comprising of the first two Sections from the book 'Healing And Freedom Through Truth Encounters.' It is a much shorter version specifically dealing with the 'Truth Encounters' ministry in isolation.

RECEIVING TRUTH THAT WILL SET YOU FREE - Steve Pidd
This booklet is designed as a basic introduction to help position those coming for a 'Truth Encounters' ministry session to understand what is involved in receiving their breakthrough.

NOTES:

www.ingramcontent.com/pod-product-compliance
Lightning Source LLC
Chambersburg PA
CBHW050321010526
44107CB00055B/2344